Unless otherwise indicated, all scripture quotes are taken from the New International Version, King James, New King James and New Living Translations of the bible.

15 14 13 12 11 10 09 08   8 7 6 5 4 3 2 1

Wildflowers A Scriptural Journal
with Painting Lesson and Inner Wisdom Questions
Original Wildflowers Watercolor

Copyright © 2024
By Bonnie McPhail

Printed in the United States of America all rights reserved under International Copyright Law. Contents and/or cover may not be reproduced in whole or in part without the express permission of the Author.

Wildflowers A Scriptural Journal
With Painting Lesson and Inner Wisdom Questions
By
Bonnie McPhail

"Love is like wildflowers; it's often found in the most unlikely places." – Ralph Waldo Emerson.

Dear Friends,

Writing your dreams, hopes, prayers and imaginations can be a powerful tool in your life.

This journal begins with an encouraging story and bible lesson and includes thought provoking questions that will give you inner wisdom. Listen as you write and you will find your answers.

The cover is an original acrylic painting that uses palette knives to create the texture and dimension. The steps are photographed and included and you can find them on page 219. In addition there are beautiful angelic messages from the heart of the Father.

Each page starts with a scripture and I promise you God will speak directly to you. He has a specific and wonderfully unique plan for your life.

May he grant every heart's desire, bring you delight, and reveal amazing truths as you work through this journal!
Blessings dear friends!
Pastor Bonnie

A Volkswagen Christmas

By

Bonnie McPhail

One of my most treasured Christmas memories comes from the first year my husband and I were married.

Being from the Midwest, he wanted to experience a true New England Christmas. We

Not being deterred in the least, Jeff shimmied up the tree. He proceeded to cut it down, about halfway from the top. There was a loud CRACK as the tree crashed to the ground. The stub of the original tree was left standing naked, top-less. It looked pretty pitiful. But that was okay; we had

our trophy! We proceeded to drag it back to our car.

We were so excited, and in such high spirits, we sang Christmas carols and laughed and talked. That is, until we got to the car. Then we realized we had one minor problem that we hadn't anticipated.

"Uh-oh," I said. "What are we going to do now?"

You see, we were driving a Volkswagen Beetle—one of the ORIGINAL ones. The kind that looks like a German helmet driving down the road. The tree was larger than our entire vehicle.

Still, Jeff was not deterred. He shoved the tree on top of the Volkswagen and managed to tie it in a zillion places. Our car looked like a giant tree with a windshield and wheels; a hairy bush, driving itself. All the way home we got astonished looks from the other drivers—not to mention honks and laughter. It was hilarious!

Did I mention the fact that we weren't just driving an original Volkswagen Beetle? We were driving an original OLD Volkswagen Beetle. Because the defroster wasn't working, every few

minutes we'd have to pull the hairy bush over beside the road to scrape the frost off the INSIDE of the windshield. But we were newlyweds. We didn't care. Love would get us through!

We finally got the tree home. We thought we heard peals of laughter from our landlords, as they watched the hairy bush drive into the driveway. But we cheerfully pulled the tree off the car—only to discover that it was way too tall to fit in our room. Jeff cut the top off, again. Now we had a stub that matched the one we'd left in the woods.

We happily decorated the tree, ignoring the fact that it had a flat top and happened to lean to the side slightly. We drank hot chocolate, treasuring wonderful memories of our first time decorating together. Then we fell into an exhausted sleep from the whole ordeal.

Sometime in the middle of the night we heard this horrendous CRASH, and woke to discover that our beloved tree had fallen over. It was all too much for me. I wept uncontrollably, while Jeff hooted with laughter.

"It's not funny!" I said through my sobs. Now I was mad because he thought it was funny.

"Stupid tree! Whose idea was this, anyway?" I yelled.

Jeff stayed up half the night nailing the tree to the wall with miles of orange rope. He stepped back and looked over his handiwork.
"That will hold it," he proudly proclaimed. We made up and went back to sleep.

A few days later, I looked out the window and saw our Volkswagen coming up the driveway. Something was sticking out of the side of it. It was too dark out to decipher what the object was.

When Jeff stepped into the apartment, he was smiling and had a tender look on his face. "Close your eyes," he whispered. When I opened them, I was astonished to find a beautiful rocking chair sitting in front of the tree. Jeff was grinning from ear to ear.
"Do you like it?" he asked.
"I LOVE IT!"

I was crying, tears of joy now. For, you see, we had just discovered that I was expecting our first child. The one thing I wanted for Christmas, but didn't think we could afford, was a chair to rock my baby in.

I sat in my rocking chair in front of our tree and was filled with thankfulness for the new life we shared. And for the husband God gave me who listened to the whispers of my heart.

I looked at the crooked, tacky tree and all I could see was the beauty of its branches and the promises it contained. I no longer saw the tangled orange rope, or the broken ornaments, or the bent limbs. I only saw my husband standing in front of it with a grin on his face, full of wonder and hope for our lives together. And the love he had for me and our unborn child shone in his eyes.

There is a special reason why I wanted to share this story with you. You see, when my husband and I were first married, the doctor told us we would never have children.

He'd also said, "If you do get pregnant, you'll never be able to carry a baby."

Because I was born twelve weeks early, all of my female organs were arranged in the wrong places. I also had an orange-sized growth on my organs.

So not only was it anatomically impossible for me to get pregnant and carry a baby, but now I was

facing surgery that would further decrease my chances.

Needless to say, Jeff and I were devastated by this news. Because I grew up in a non-Christian home, the one thing I'd always longed for was having a family of my own who served the Lord. I already had the husband of my dreams; but were we destined not to have children?

One day I was reading my Bible and praying about the situation. I stumbled on a couple of Scriptures that captured my attention. In fact, it felt as if they just leapt off the page:

"Let all the earth fear the LORD; let all the people of the world revere him. For he spoke, and it came to be; he commanded, and it stood firm" (Psalm 33:8-9).

Verse 8 speaks of revering the Lord; verse 9 was specifically related to my situation. The Lord promised to speak into being something which didn't exist; He would command it to stand firm.

One year later I held my first born son in my arms. God is true to his word!

Perhaps, like me, you've found that God will use His Word to address specific issues in our

lives. He might speak through a friend, too, or a situation. When He speaks, you will know it. His

message will bear witness with your spirit. We must learn to recognize that message and acknowledge that He sent it.
Remember: GOD HAS A MIRACLE FOR YOU!

Bible Lesson
Believe

"And all things, whatsoever ye shall ask in prayer, believing, ye shall receive." Matthew 21:22

Did you know that God has made a way for you to receive the most impossible answers to prayer? Did you know that he wants you to believe him for the most impossible circumstances in your life? That he truly is big enough?

I have experienced this many times in my own life and I am still after all these years ever learning, ever searching, ever BELIEVING!

In my early years as a young wife I desperately longed to have a baby of my own. The doctor told me it was anatomically impossible and that even if I got pregnant I would never be able to carry a baby.

Standing on the word of God became a powerful truth in my life. I found a verse and stood on it, speaking it out loud every day. One year after I stood on the word I held my first born son in my arms. Not only did God answer my prayer for one he actually gave me four! God always goes above and beyond anything we could ever think or imagine.

I decided to teach you how to stand on God's word for the biggest most impossible things in your life. I will be doing it too right along with you. Are you ready? Lets get started!

The first place we will begin will be doing some soul searching to uncover the impossible circumstances in our lives, what is hindering our dreams, what and who might be limiting what God wants to accomplish in our lives.

Take a few moments to write down the answers to these questions. This is a time to be brutally honest. Ask the Lord to reveal what needs to be revealed and expose what is hidden. There is true freedom in this.

1. If you could ask God for anything what would it be?

_____
_____
_____
_____
_____
_____
_____
_____

2. If money were no object what would your life look like?

4. What limits you?

5. Who limits you? Why?

_____
_____
_____
_____
_____
_____
_____
_____
_____

6. Is there something from your past that has caused you to be afraid to believe God?

_____
_____
_____
_____
_____
_____
_____
_____
_____

7. Who do you need to forgive? Why?

8. What brings you joy and fulfillment?

9. What is the biggest need you have now?

10. What is the most impossible thing in your life that you are believing God for?

We are now going to take a moment to pour out our hearts to Jesus. Write out everything that is on your heart, all the joys, losses, fears, dreams. Tell the Lord exactly how you feel and why.

Dear Jesus,

"God charts the road you take."
Psalm 1:6 MSG

"Jesus said, "Throw your lot in with the One that God has sent. That kind of commitment gets you in on God's works."
John 6:29 MSG

"Every time we think of you, we thank God for you. Day and night your in our prayers."
       1 Thessalonians 1:2 MSG

What is it you love to do?

1._____

_____

2._____

_____

3._____

_____

4._____

_____

New Opportunities

Let excitement arise in your heart, for this is a time of newness, restoration, and a time for the harvest of seeds that have been planted long ago.

It is also a season of fresh vision, and new opportunities; all that has been before is for such a time as this. There shall be great rejoicing because of it.

Scripture
"For the Lord is a sun and shield; the Lord bestows favor and honor;
no good thing does He withhold from those whose walk is blameless."
Psalm 84:11 NIV

*"God's a safe-house for the battered,
a sanctuary during bad times."*
Psalm 9:9 MSG

"Jesus said, "I am the bread of life. The person who aligns with me hungers no more, ever."
John 6:35 MSG

"May God our Father himself and our Master Jesus clear the road to you!"
1 Thessalonians 3:11 MSG

What makes you smile?

1._____

_____

2._____

_____

3._____

_____

4._____

_____

5._____

_____

6._____

_____

Endurance

Run the race I have set before you. Run and do not be weary

for I will give you strength and endurance. I will provide whatever you need along the way. I bring peace, love, joy and restoration.

Scripture

"Revive us, and we will call upon your name. Restore us, O Lord God of hosts; cause your face to shine, and we shall be saved."

Psalm 81:18 N.I.V

"Now you've got my feet on the life path, all radiant from the shining of your face. Ever since you took my hand, I'm on the right way. Psalm 16:11 MSG

"I'm staying on your trail; I'm putting one foot in front of the other. I'm not giving up."
Psalm 17:4 MSG

"Then you will experience for yourselves the truth, and the truth will free you."
John 8:32 MSG

What do you feel you were born to do?

1. _____

2. _____

3. _____

4. _____

5. _____

6. _____

7. _____

8. _____

9. _____

10. _____

11. _____

12. _____

Giving

Whatever you lack, give. Love? - Give it away. Forgiveness? - Give that too. Finances? - Sow seeds of money. Whatever you sow you will reap.

Spiritual seed given from a heart of faith, trust, and love without expecting anything in return; will reap a mighty spiritual harvest. So give out of your need, and watch what I will do!

Scripture
"Give and it will be given to you: good measure, pressed down, shaken together, and running over will be put into your bosom. For with the same measure that you use, it will be measured back to you."
Luke 6:38 NKJV

*"So if the son sets you free,
you are free through and through."*
John 8:36 MSG

"God is bedrock under my feet, the castle in which I live, my rescuing knight." Psalm 18:2

"May you be infused with strength and purity, filled with confidence in the presence of God our Father..." 1 Thessalonians 3:13 MSG

What do you do best?

1. _____
2. _____
3. _____
4. _____
5. _____
6. _____
7. _____
8. _____
9. _____
10. _____
11. _____
12. _____

Faithful

    I am faithful to do for you just as I have promised. Hold fast to what I have shown you. Do not waiver. Let not the circumstances discourage or detour you. For I am with you. I am greatly at work. Peace be still, all is well.

Scripture
"Let us old fast the confession of our hope without wavering,
for He who promised is faithful."
Hebrews 10:23 NKJV

"The One who called you is completely dependable. If he said it, he'll do it!"
1 Thessalonians 5:24 MSG

"God made my life complete when I placed all the pieces before him. When I got my act together, he gave me a fresh start." Psalm 18:20 MSG

"The gatekeeper opens the gate to him and the sheep recognize his voice. He calls his own sheep by name and leads them out."
John 10:2 T.M.

What can you do with little effort?

1. _____

2. _____

3. _____

4. _____

5. _____

6. _____

7. _____

8. _____

9. _____

10. _____

Peaceful Streams

You can tell when I am the one leading you for when I lead you it brings peace. If you do not have peace in your life, then consider who the one leading is. Is it you? Or is the enemy of your soul? Remember the shepherd is the one who brings peace and rest.

Scripture

He lets me rest in green meadows; he leads me beside peaceful streams."

Psalm 23:2 N.L.T

"Everything God created is good, and to be received with thanks. Nothing is to be sneered and thrown out." 1 Timothy 4:4 MSG

"What a God! His road stretches straight and smooth."
Psalm 18:30 MSG

"Every God-direction is road-tested. Everyone who runs toward him makes it."
Psalm 18:30 MSG

What areas in your life are you naturally strong?

1. _____
2. _____
3. _____
4. _____
5. _____
6. _____
7. _____
8. _____
9. _____
10. _____
11. _____

Sow Generously

There is a kingdom principle about sowing and reaping that will be a powerful force in your life. This is the secret; whatever kinds of seeds you sow are the kinds of harvest that will be produced. Sow seeds of love, kindness, gentleness and patience and when you need those things they shall be given. Sow seeds of your material resources. Give and it shall be given to you pressed down and running over that you shall not be able to contain it. Sow generously and generously you shall receive.

Scripture

"Remember the farmer who plants only a few seeds will get a small crop. But the one who plants generously will get a generous crop."

II Corinthians 9:6 N.L.T.

"A devout life brings wealth, but it's the rich simplicity of being yourself before God."
1 Timothy 6:6 MSG

"God's glory is on tour in the skies, God-craft on exhibit across the horizon."
Psalm 19:1 MSG

"Tune your ears to the world of Wisdom; set your heart on a life of understanding."
Proverbs 2:2 MSG

What has helped you get where you are today?

1. _____

2. _____

3. _____

4. _____

5. _____

6. _____

7. _____

8. _____

9. _____

10. _____

11. _____

12. _____

Gracious

Humility is not being lowly and taken advantage of by others or not being able to speak honestly from a heart of love, no humility is knowing that your absolute faith and trust is in me, and the ability that comes from doing all in my strength not yours. This is true humility and it opens the doors for my grace to abound in your life.

Scripture

"But (the Lord) is gracious to the humble." Proverbs 3:34b N.L.T.

"Earn a reputation for living well in God's eyes and the eyes of the people."
Proverbs 3:4 MSG

"I am the good shepherd. I know my own sheep and my own sheep know me."
John 10:14 MSG

*"Send reinforcements from Holy Hill, Dispatch
from Zion fresh supplies."*
Psalm 20:2 MSG

What skills will help you attain your future goals?

1. _____
2. _____
3. _____
4. _____
5. _____
6. _____
7. _____
8. _____
9. _____
10. _____
11. _____
12. _____

Integrity

When you know my name I will guide you into all truth and the paths before you shall be made straight and wide, keeping your foot from falling.

Scripture

"People with integrity walk safely, but those who follow crooked paths will slip and fall."

Proverbs 10:9 NLT

"If anyone of you wants to serve me, then follow me. Then you'll be where I am, ready to serve at a moment's notice. The Father will honor and reward anyone who serves me."
John 12:26 MSG

_____

_____

_____

_____

_____

_____

_____

_____

"That clinches it-help's coming, an answer's on the way, everything's going to work out."
Psalm 20:6 MSG

*"Trust God from the bottom of your heart;
don't try to figure out everything on your own."*
Proverbs 3:5 MSG

What excites you and gets you out of bed?

1. _____
2. _____
3. _____
4. _____
5. _____
6. _____
7. _____
8. _____
9. _____
10. _____
11. _____
12. _____

Long Life

Think about those times when your mouth is full of my praises; it makes you feel happy and joyful on the inside. On the other hand a mouth that is full of complaining and curses brings depression, lack of faith and doubts. This leads to stress, anxiety and worry which are enemies. Learn instead to use your mouth to say good things and you will have a long and healthy life.

Scripture

"Those who control their tongue will have a long life; opening your mouth can ruin everything." Proverbs 10:9 NLT

*"Down and outers sit at
God's table and eat their fill."
Psalm 22:26 MSG*

"Listen for God's voice in everything you do, everywhere you go; he's the one who will keep you on track." Proverbs 3:6 MSG

"Make sure you get this right: receiving someone I send is the same as receiving me, just as receiving me is the same as receiving the one who sent me." John 13:20 MSG

What part of tomorrow excites you?

1. _____
2. _____
3. _____
4. _____
5. _____
6. _____
7. _____
8. _____
9. _____
10. _____
11. _____
12. _____

Wonderfully Made

You are fearfully and wonderfully made. Just as I knew you while you were being formed; so I know you now. I have good and wonderful plans for your life. My plans and purposes bring growth, mercy, love and provision.

All that you have need of, I will supply. Seek me with all of your heart, and you will be greatly blessed. I reward those who diligently seek me.

Scripture

"You saw me before I was born. Every day of my life was recorded in your book. How precious are your thoughts about me O God. They cannot be numbered." Psalm 139:9 N.I.V

*"Let me give you a new command: Love one another. In the same way I loved you,
you love one another." John 13:34 MSG*

"Even when the goes through Death Valley, I'm not afraid when you walk at my side. Your trusty shepherd's crook makes me feel secure."
Psalm 23:4 MSG

"You serve me a six course dinner right in front of my enemies. You revive my drooping head; my cup brims with blessing." Psalm 23:5 MSG

_____

_____

_____

_____

_____

_____

_____

_____

_____

_____

What fulfills you?

1. _____
2. _____
3. _____
4. _____
5. _____
6. _____
7. _____
8. _____
9. _____
10. _____
11. _____
12. _____

Hope

I know the ashes you have in your life. I know the times you have felt hopeless, depressed, and weary. I have heard your cries. Understand that my mercies are new every morning, you have only to ask.

I will turn your mourning into dancing. Through the misery you have suffered, I will take all of it and use it for my glory; to strengthen and enlighten you. It is my promise to you to turn all things out for your good. Let go of the past, trust me, I am well able to do more than you can imagine.

Scripture "He will give a crown of beauty for ashes; a joyous blessing instead of mourning, festive praise instead of despair."
Isaiah 61:3 NLT

"Honor God with everything you own; give him the first and the best."
Proverbs 3:9 MSG

"Mark the milestones of your mercy and love, God; Rebuild the ancient landmarks!"
Psalm 25:6 MSG

*"Keep vigilant watch over your heart;
that's where life starts."*
Proverbs 4:23 MSG

What is something you always wanted to be extraordinary at?

1. _____
2. _____
3. _____
4. _____
5. _____
6. _____
7. _____
8. _____
9. _____
10. _____
11. _____
12. _____

Dream

Dare to believe in your hopes and in your dreams; for I have put them within you. There are endless possibilities in them. My entire heavenly host is at your disposal, you have only to ask. All that was and is to come; and all that will be today belong to you. Just dare to dream.

Scripture

"It is God who arms me with strength and makes my way perfect. He makes my feet like the feet of a deer he enables me to stand on the heights."

Psalm 18:32 N.I.V

*"Keep vigilant watch over your heart;
That's where life starts."*
Proverbs 4:23 MSG

_____

_____

_____

_____

_____

_____

_____

_____

_____

_____

"From now on every road you travel will take you to God. Follow the covenant signs; read the charted directions." Psalm 25:10 MSG

"God friendship is for God worshipers; they are the ones he confides in." Psalm 25:14 MSG

What part of your work do you love?

1._____

2._____

3._____

4._____

5._____

6._____

7._____

8._____

9._____

10._____

11._____

12._____

Success

I the Lord am with you. It is my desire to bless you in all that you do.

Seek my face, spend time with me. It is here in the stillness of the moment;

and the quietness of the day, that you will find my will and my purposes for your life. Put me first in all things and everything you do will be successful.

Scripture

"In everything he did he had great success, because the Lord was with him."

1 Samuel 18:14 NIV

"God holds me head and shoulders above all who try to pull me down. I'm headed for his place to offer anthems that will raise the roof!"
Psalm 27:6 MSG

"Point me down your highway, God; direct me along a well lighted street; show my enemies whose side you're on" Psalm 27:11 MSG

"I'm sure now I'll see God's goodness in the exuberant earth." Psalm 27:13 MSG

When you leave this earth, what will you feel better knowing you have accomplished? How?

1. _____

2. _____

3. _____

4. _____

5. _____

6. _____

7. _____

8. _____

9. _____

10. _____

11. _____

12. _____

Laughter and Joy

"Laughter and joy are my gifts to you. Enjoy them; seek them, and embrace them. Let them fill you to overflowing and splash on all those I will send you.

They will bring health and well-being. Life is good and I send good gifts to you. So laugh my child and be merry!

Scripture

"A merry heart does good like a medicine." Proverbs 17:22 N.K.J.V

"If you love me, show it by doing what I've told you." John 14:15 MSG

"God is all strength for his people, ample refuge for his chosen leader." Psalm 28:8 MSG

*"Watch your step, and the road will
Stretch out smooth before you."*
Proverbs 4:26 MSG

What would you like to do more of in your life?

1. _____
2. _____
3. _____
4. _____
5. _____
6. _____
7. _____
8. _____
9. _____
10. _____
11. _____
12. _____

Believe

For I tell you, that nothing is impossible with me. I am well able to meet every need that you have. There is nothing that I can't help you handle.

All things are possible. Nothing is too big for me; my promises are true.

Just believe...

Scripture

"If you can believe all things are possible to him who believes."

Mark 9:23 NKJV

"But, if you make yourselves at home with me and my words at home in you, you can be sure that whatever you ask will be listened to and acted upon." John 15:7 MSG

"I Give you all the credit, God you got me out of that mess, you didn't let my enemies gloat."
Psalm 30:1 MSG

*"I love those who love me;
Those who look for me find me"*
Proverbs 8:17 MSG

What is your next level of development?

1. _____
2. _____
3. _____
4. _____
5. _____
6. _____
7. _____
8. _____
9. _____
10. _____
11. _____
12. _____

Kindness

Be kind to everyone you come in contact with today for you do not know how deeply you will touch a life. When you are kind to others from a pure heart, not seeking to be seen of others; I tell you great are your rewards!

Scripture

"I will tell of the kindness of the Lord, for the deeds for which he is to be praised, according to all the Lord has done for us."
Psalm 63:7 NIV

*"Handing out life to those who love me,
Filling their arms with life arm loads of life!*
Proverbs 8:21 MSG

"You did it: you changed wild lament into whirling dance; you ripped off my black mourning band and decked me with wildflowers."
Psalm 30:11 T.M.

"I'm about to burst with song; I can't keep quiet about you. God; my God, I can't thank you enough."
Psalm 30:12 MSG

What though makes you the happiest? Why?

1. _____
2. _____
3. _____
4. _____
5. _____
6. _____
7. _____
8. _____
9. _____
10. _____
11. _____
12. _____

Beloved

I am the author of all that is good, and lovely, and pure in your life. I am love! I love you more than you can imagine. I bring good gifts to my children. You have only to ask. Prove me and see if I will not pour out a blessing!

Scripture

"Love never fails…"

1 Corinthians 13:8 NKJV

"Haven't I commanded you? Strength! Courage! Don't be timid; don't get discouraged. GOD, you God, is with you every step you take."
Joshua 1:9 MSG

"I've put my life in your hands. Don't drop me, you'll never let me down." Psalm 31:5 MSG

*"I'm leaping and singing in the circle of y our love;
you saw my pain, you disarmed my tormentors."*
Psalm 31:7 MSG

What are your strengths?

1. _____
2. _____
3. _____
4. _____
5. _____
6. _____
7. _____
8. _____
9. _____
10. _____

Faith

Let faith arise in your heart. I have heard your prayers. I am at work in ways that you cannot understand or fathom. Believe my word. Let it arise in your heart. When you learn to stand on my word and listen to the voice of my spirit, I will give you the certainty of what you are believing for.

Scripture

"Now faith is being sure of what we hope for and certain of what we do not see." Hebrews 11:1 NIV

"God, you God, gives you rest and he gives you this land." Joshua 1:13 MSG

"Guard my common good: Do what's right and do it in the right way, for salvation is just around the corner, my setting things right is about to go into action." Isaiah 56:1 MSG

"Blessed God! His love is the wonder of the world." Psalm 31:21 MSG

What would motivate you to tap your strengths?

1. _____
2. _____
3. _____
4. _____
5. _____
6. _____
7. _____
8. _____
9. _____
10. _____
11. _____
12. _____

Prayer

Pray as you go about the mundane tasks of your day. Be instant in season and out of season. You do not realize the fearsome battles which are raged, nor broken hearts mended, or the bountiful blessings which are provided. I will still the storm to a whisper, and send my angels. If you will but believe, and pray my word, I am waiting to answer."

Scripture

"Therefore I tell you, whatever you ask for in prayer, believe that you have received it, and it will be yours." Mark 11:22 NIV

"I know what I'm doing. I have it all planned out plans to take care of you, not abandon you, plans to give you the future to hope for."
Jeremiah 29:11

"Count yourself lucky, how happy you must be you get a fresh start, your slate's wiped clean."
Psalm 32:1 MSG

"Count yourself lucky-God holds nothing against you and your holding nothing back from him."
Psalm 32:2 MSG

What does not satisfy you about you?

1. _____
2. _____
3. _____
4. _____
5. _____
6. _____
7. _____
8. _____
9. _____
10. _____
11. _____
12. _____

"When you call on me, when you coma and pray to me, I'll listen." Her 29:12 to me, I'll listen."

"Celebrate God. Sing together everyone! All you honest hearts, raise the roof! Psalm 32:11 MSG

"Invent your own new song to him; give him a trumpet fanfare." Psalm 33:3 MSG

What energizes and inspires you?

1. _____
2. _____
3. _____
4. _____
5. _____
6. _____
7. _____
8. _____
9. _____
10. _____
11. _____
12. _____

Hearts Desires

It is my good pleasure to grant your hearts desires, for the ones that are truly of me will bring you health, love, joy and peace.

Seek after me with all your heart and I will be known to you. I long to give you an abundant life.

Scripture

Take delight in the Lord and he will give you your heart's desires."

Psalm 37:4 NLT

"When you come looking for me, you'll find me. Yes, when you get serious about finding me and want it more than anything else, I'll make sure you won't be disappointed."
Jeremiah 29:13 MSG

"The skies were made by God's command; he breathed the word and stars popped out."
Psalm 33:6 T.M.

"He spoke and there it was, in place the moment he said so." Psalm 33:9 MSG

What is the best part of your day now?

1. _____
2. _____
3. _____
4. _____
5. _____
6. _____
7. _____
8. _____
9. _____
10. _____
11. _____
12. _____

Love

I am the author of faith, hope, and love. Nothing is too big for me to handle. Cast all your cares on me for I care for you. I am with you no matter what you face. I will make a way for you. Trust me.

Scripture

"Love never gives up, never loses faith, is always hopeful, and endures through every circumstance."

1 Corinthians 13:3 NLT

"Most of all, love each other as if your life depended on it. Love makes up for practically anything." 1Peter 4:8 MSG

"Be generous with the different things God gave you, passing them around so all get in on it."
1Peter 4:10 MSG

*"If words, let it be God's words; if help,
let it be God's hearty help."*
1 Peter 4:11 MSG

If money were no object what would your life be like?

1. _____
2. _____
3. _____
4. _____
5. _____
6. _____
7. _____
8. _____
9. _____
10. _____

Give Thanks to the Lord

    Praise and thanksgiving are two of the most powerful tools I have given you.
Use them. Praise me and watch what I will do in your life! Do not try to do anything in your own strength. Look to me with your whole heart and I will give you strength. Remember nothing is impossible and I will work all things out for your good.

Scripture
"Give thanks to the Lord, call on his name; make known among the nations what he has done. Sing praises to him; tell of his wonderful acts. Glory in his holy name; let the hearts of those who seek the Lord rejoice. Look to the Lord and his strength; seek his face and always, remember the wonders he has done, his miracles
and the rulings he has given."
Psalm 105:1-5 MSG

"Friends, when life gets really difficult, don't jump to the conclusion that God isn't on the job. Instead, be glad that you are in the very thick of what Christ experienced. This is a spiritual refining process, with glory just around the corner." 1 Peter 4:12,13 MSG

"So if you find life difficult because you're doing what God said, take it in stride. Trust him. He knows what he's doing, and he'll keep on doing it." 1 Peter 4:19 MSG

"So be content with who you are, and don't put on airs. God's strong hand is on you; he'll promote you at the right time." 1Peter 5:6 MSG

Close your eyes. What do you see?

1. _____

2. _____

3. _____

4. _____

5. _____

6. _____

7. _____

8. _____

9. _____

10. _____

11. _____

12. _____

Shepherd

I am gently leading and guiding you. I know what you have need of before you even ask. Take heart, for I will carry you through whatever you face to the lovely green pastures of peace, provision and plenty.

Scripture
"The Lord is my shepherd, I shall lack nothing. He makes me lie down in green pastures, he leads me beside quiet waters, he restores my soul, he guides me in the paths of righteousness for his name's sake. Even though I walk through the valley of the shadow of death, I will fear no evil for you are with me; your rod and your staff, they comfort me. You prepare a table before me in the presence of my enemies. You anoint my head with oil; my cup overflows. Surely goodness and love will follow me all the days of my life, and I will dwell
in the house of the Lord forever."
Psalm 23 NIV

*"Live carefree before God;
he is most careful with you."* 1 Peter 5:7 MSG

"Love us, God, with all you've got that's what we're depending on." Psalm 33:22 MSG

"I bless God every chance I get; my lungs expand with his praise. I live and breathe God."
Psalm 43:1,2 MSG

What would make your life extraordinary?

1. _____

2. _____

3. _____

4. _____

5. _____

6. _____

7. _____

8. _____

9. _____

10. _____

*"Look at him; give him your warmest smile.
Never hide your feelings from him."*

Psalm 34:5 MSG

_____

_____

_____

_____

_____

_____

_____

_____

_____

_____

*"When I was desperate, I called out,
and God got me out of a tight spot."*
Psalm 34:6 MSG

"God's angel sets up a circle of protection around us while we pray."
Psalm 34:7 MSG

Where would you choose to live and work?

1. _____
2. _____
3. _____
4. _____
5. _____
6. _____
7. _____
8. _____
9. _____
10. _____

Angel of Protection

There is a great host at your disposal you have only to ask. It is my great pleasure to protect, guide, direct, and assist you in every aspect of your life.

I am closer than you can imagine. Cry out to me and I will listen; ask me to help you and so I shall. I will never leave you or forsake you.

Scripture

"For the angel of the Lord is a guard; he surrounds and defends all who fear him."

Psalm 34:7 NLT

"Worship God if you want the best; worship opens doors to all his goodness."
Psalm 34:8 MSG

"Worship God if you want the best; worship opens doors to all his goodness."
Psalm 34:9 MSG

*"Is anyone crying for help?
God is listening, ready to rescue you."*
Psalm 34:17 MSG

What is your vision of your perfect life?

1. _____
2. _____
3. _____
4. _____
5. _____
6. _____
7. _____
8. _____
9. _____
10. _____

Plans

Let go of the past and embrace the present, look forward to the future.

I am doing a new work in your life. Enjoy today, and discover that there is joy in serving others.

Scripture

"For I know the plans I have for you." Says the Lord. "They are plans for good and not for disaster, to give you a future and a hope. In those days when you pray I will listen. If you look for me wholeheartedly, you will find me."
Jeremiah 29:11 NIV

"I'll turn things around for you."

Jeremiah 29:14 MSG

"God, there's no one like you. You put the down and out on their feet and protect the unprotected from bullies." Psalm 35:9, 10 MSG

"I'll tell the world how great and good you are, I'll shout Hallelujah all day, every day."
Psalm 35:28 MSG

What would make your life better now?

1. _____

2. _____

3. _____

4. _____

5. _____

6. _____

7. _____

8. _____

9. _____

10. _____

Courage

Courage is my gift to you to equip you to take the land I have given you. Hold fast to the dreams I have placed in your heart. Stay the course, and dare to do great exploits in my name. I go before you, and I will pave the way. Let not your heart be troubled, neither let it be afraid for I am with you.

Scripture

"Have not I commanded you? Be strong and of good courage; do not be afraid or dismayed, for the Lord your God is with you wherever you go." Joshua 1:9 NIV

*"You're a fountain of cascading light,
and you open our eyes to light."*
Psalm 36:9 MSG

*"Keep on loving your friends;
Do your work in welcoming hearts."*
Psalm 36:10 MSG

"And then I'll enter the darkness. I'll break the yoke from their necks, cut them loose from the harness." Jeremiah 30:8 MSG

What action can you take today?

1. _____

2. _____

3. _____

4. _____

5. _____

6. _____

7. _____

8. _____

9. _____

10. _____

Cares

I am the author of faith, hope, and love. Nothing is too big for me to handle. Cast all your cares on me for I care for you. I am with you no matter what you face. I will make a way for you. Trust me.

Scripture

"Love never gives up, never loses faith, is always hopeful, and endures through every circumstance." 1 Corinthians 13:3 NLT

"Quiet down before God, be prayerful before him. Don't bother with those who climb the ladder, who elbow their way to the top." Psalm 37:7 TM

"God keeps track of the decent folk; what they do won't soon be forgotten."
Psalm 37:18 MSG

*"In hard times, they'll hold their heads high;
when the shelves are bare, they'll be full."*
Psalm 37:19 MSG

What are your most fulfilling accomplishments?

1. _____
2. _____
3. _____
4. _____
5. _____
6. _____
7. _____
8. _____
9. _____
10. _____

*"Stalwart walks in step with God;
His path blazed by God, he's happy."*
Psalm 37:23 MSG

*"If he stumbles, he's not down for long;
God has a grip on his hand."*
Psalm 37:24 MSG

"Turn your back on evil, Work for good and don't quit." Psalm 37:27 MSG

What is your greatest asset?

1. _____
2. _____
3. _____
4. _____
5. _____
6. _____
7. _____
8. _____
9. _____
10. _____
11. _____
12. _____

Promise

You can trust me to keep my promises. I am not a man that I should lie. My promises are true and lasting, even to future generations. Trust me to do as I have said. I will keep my word to you. Hold fast to my promises; and the dreams I have placed in your heart.

Scripture

"So is my word that goes out from my mouth: It will not return to me empty, but will accomplish what I desire and achieve the purpose for which I sent it."

Isaiah 56:11 NIV

"Wait patiently for God, don't leave the path. He'll give you your place in the sun while you watch the wicked lose it." Psalm 37:34 MSG

"The spacious, free life from God, It's protected and safe." Psalm 37:39 T.M.

"God strengthened, we're delivered from evil when we run to him, he saves us."
Psalm 37:40 MSG

What have you accomplished in the past?

1. _____
2. _____
3. _____
4. _____
5. _____
6. _____
7. _____
8. _____
9. _____
10. _____

Trust

Let not your heart be troubled, neither let it be afraid for I the Lord am with you. Trust me with the simplicity of a little child. Let there be the wonder of love, laughter and surprises! For I give good gifts to you. I have your very best in mind. I am at work. Trust me...

Scripture

"Do not let your hearts be troubled. Trust in God; trust also in me."

John 14:1 NIV

"He taught me how to sing the latest God song, a praise song to our God. More and more people are seeing this: They enter the mystery, abandoning themselves to God."
Psalm 40:3 MSG

"Blessed are you who give yourselves over to God, turn your backs on the world's "sure thin," ignore what the world worships."
Psalm 40:4 MSG

"But all who are hunting for you, let them sing and be happy. Let those who know what you're all about tell the world you're great and not quitting." Psalm 40:16 MSG

What are you good at?

1. _____
2. _____
3. _____
4. _____
5. _____
6. _____
7. _____
8. _____
9. _____
10. _____

Peace

My peace I give to you, not as the world give do I give to you. My peace goes down into all the wounded, hurting and broken pieces of your tattered heart.

My peace gives you rest in the storm, strength for the trial, and an unspeakable inner calm.

Rest in it, and relax in the comfort of it.

Peace be still my precious one, all is well.

Scripture

"You will keep in perfect peace him whose mind is steadfast,

because he trusts in you."

Isaiah 26:3 NIV

"A white tailed deer drinks from the creek; I want to drink God, deep draughts of God."
Psalm 42:1 MSG

"Why are you down in the dumps, dear soul? Why are you crying the blues? Fix my eyes on God soon I'll be praising again. He puts a smile on my face. He's my God." Psalm 42:5 MSG

*"Then God promises to love me all day, sing songs all through the night!
My life is God's prayer.
Psalm 42:8 MSG*

What are you putting up with? Why?

1. _____
2. _____
3. _____
4. _____
5. _____
6. _____
7. _____
8. _____
9. _____
10. _____

Patience

Have patience, and trust in me, even though you do not always understand. Remember my ways are higher than yours. I will work all things out for your good. Those who wait upon me shall renew their strength. Patience produces a great harvest. Wait on me, and watch what I will do.

Scripture

"For whatever things were written before were written for our learning, that we through patience and comfort of the scriptures might have hope."

Romans 15:4 NKJV

"We didn't fight for this land; we didn't work for it-it was a gift! You gave it, smiling as you gave it, delighting as you gave it." Psalm 44:3 MSG

"God is a safe place to hide, ready to help when we need him. We stand fearless at the cliff edge of doom, courageous in seastorm and earthquake."
Psalm 46:1,2 MSG

"Before the rush and roar of oceans, the tremors that shift mountains. Jacob-wrestling God fights for us, God of angel armies protects us."
Psalm 46:3 MSG

What are your blessings?

1. _____
2. _____
3. _____
4. _____
5. _____
6. _____
7. _____
8. _____
9. _____
10. _____

Beautiful

All that is beautiful and good I bring into your life. All that is cherished

comes from me. My gift to you. You are treasured and loved dearly.

My blessings are upon you.

Scripture

"He has made all things beautiful in his time."

Ecclesiastes 3:11 NIV

"Be glad, Zion Mountain; Dance, Judah's daughter! He does what he said he'd do!"
Psalm 48:11 MSG

"Generous in love God, give grace! Huge in mercy wipe out my bad record."
Psalm 51:1 MSG

"I'm absolutely convinced that nothing living or dead, angelic or demonic, today or tomorrow, high or low, thinkable or unthinkable absolutely nothing can get between us and God's love."
Romans 8:38 MSG

What are your possibilities?

1. _____

2. _____

3. _____

4. _____

5. _____

6. _____

7. _____

8. _____

9. _____

10. _____

Faith

Let faith arise in your heart. I have heard your prayers. I am at work in ways that you cannot understand or fathom. Believe my word, let it arise in your heart. When you learn to stand upon my word, and listen to the voice of my spirit, I will give you the certainty of what you are believing for.

Scripture

"Now faith is being sure of what we hope for and certain of what we do not see."

Hebrews 11:1 NIV

*"Oh, look! God's right here helping!
God's on my side."*
Psalm 54:4 MSG

*"I'm ready now to worship, so ready.
I thank you, God you're so good."*
Psalm 54:6 MSG

*"Come close and whisper your answer.
I really need you."*
Psalm 55:2 MSG

What are your dreams?

1. _____
2. _____
3. _____
4. _____
5. _____
6. _____
7. _____
8. _____
9. _____
10. _____

Secrets of the Heart

For I know the plans I have for you says the Lord, plans for good and not for evil, plans to give you a future and a hope. My divine purposes are unfolding. Rest in that. I will not leave you stranded or helpless. Find the joy in what I have called you to do. Find the joy even today. Now is the time to bring forth all those secret, hidden desires and dreams I have placed in your heart.

Scripture

"But seek first his kingdom and his righteousness and all these things will be given to you as well." Mathew 6:33 NIV

"That's why we can be so sure that every detail in our lives of love for Go is worked into something good."
Romans 8:28 MSG

"My life is well and whole, secure in the middle of danger even while thousands are lined up against me." Psalm 55:18 MSG

"Pile your troubles on God's shoulders he'll carry your load, he'll help you out. He'll never let good people topple into ruin." Psalm 55:22 MSG

What action can you take towards your dreams?

1. _____
2. _____
3. _____
4. _____
5. _____
6. _____
7. _____
8. _____
9. _____
10. _____

Today

Don't worry about all the tomorrows, just enjoy today. My plans and purposes are unfolding. Trust in Me. No matter what happens I am here with you. My grace is sufficient and I am at work in every situation. I work all things out for your good.

Scripture

"I will lead the blind along ways they have not known. Along unfamiliar paths I will guide them; I will turn the darkness into light and make the rough places smooth. These are the things I will do. I will not forsake them."

Isaiah 42:16 – 17 NIV

"I'm proud to praise God, proud to praise God. Fearless now, I trust in God; what can mere mortals do to me? Psalm 56:10,11 MSG

"God, you did everything you promised, and I'm thanking you with all my heart."
Psalm 56:12 MSG

"You pulled me from the brink of death, my feet from the cliff edge of doom. Now I stroll at leisure with God in my sunlit fields of life."
Psalm 56:13 MSG

What matters most to you?

1. _____
2. _____
3. _____
4. _____
5. _____
6. _____
7. _____
8. _____
9. _____
10. _____

Stand

Stand fast. Hold tight to what I have shown you. I will make a way in the wilderness and streams in the desert shall be provided for you; for I am with you. I am greatly at work in the most difficult circumstances in your life. Hold my hand and stand.

Scripture

"You will not need to fight this battle, position yourselves, stand still and see the salvation of the Lord, who dwells with you."

2 Chronicles 20:17 NKJV

*"I call out to High God,
The God who holds me together."*
Psalm 57:2 MSG

"He sends orders from heaven and saves me, he humiliates those who kick me around. God delivers generous love, he makes good on his word."
Psalm 57:3 MSG

_____

_____

_____

_____

_____

_____

_____

_____

_____

*"Soar high in the skies, O God!
Cover the whole earth with your glory!"*
Psalm 57:5 MSG

How can your life bring God glory?

1. _____
2. _____
3. _____
4. _____
5. _____
6. _____
7. _____
8. _____
9. _____
10. _____

Refuge

I am your refuge, I am your strength. I am with you in the midst of all that troubles you.

Fear not, though tumultuous times are all around you.

I am greater than these. I will keep you safe, tucked up under my wings,

safe, warm, and greatly loved.

Scripture

God is our refuge and strength, a very present help in trouble."

Psalm 46:1 NKJV

About the Author/Artist:

Bonnie McPhail is an ordained Minister with certifications in Life Coaching and Pastoral Studies, along with a BS in Organizational Management and AS in Nursing.

Here is the print I was telling you about. You can either tear out the page or cut it out and frame it.

For this is how God loved the world: He gave his one and only Son, so that everyone who believes in him will not perish but have eternal life. God sent his son into the world not to judge the world, but to save the world through him." John 3:16 NLT

Ask Jesus into your heart he will give you new life! He loves you!

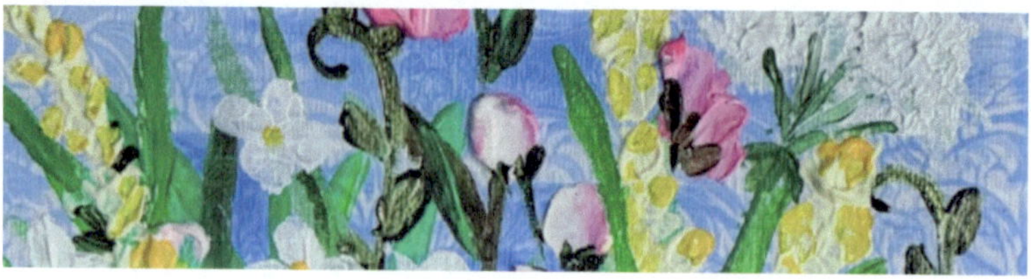

Step 1

We will be using sand yellow for the background.

Step 2

We will also be using white for the background

Step 3

Stretched 8 x 10 Canvas

Step 4

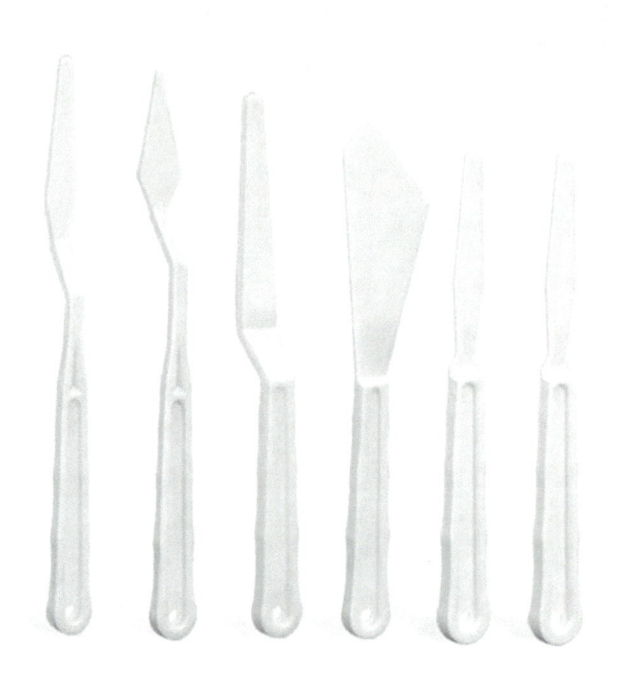

These are the palette knives we will be using. They are super expensive and can be purchased online.

Step 5

The acrylic paints can be purchased at any craft store or online. They are very affordable.

Step 6

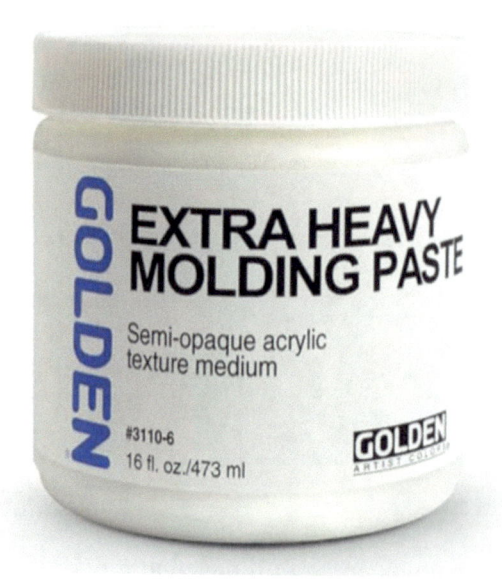

This is the secret ingredient to making the 3 dimensional textured acrylic paintings. You just take a small amount of it and mix it with whatever color you want and use the palette knife instead of a paintbrush.

Step 7

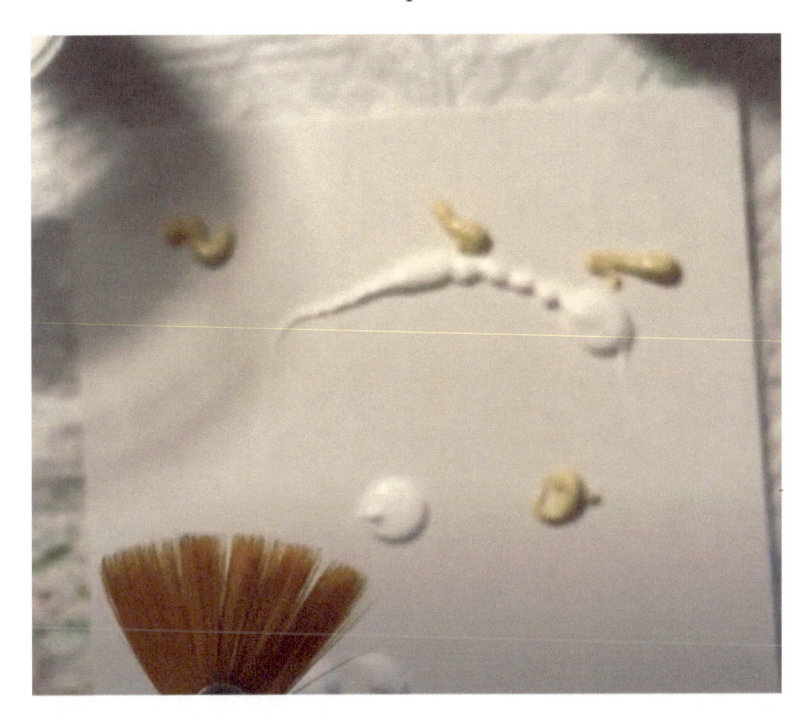

Alternate the white and ochre paint and we will be using a fan brush to spread it across the canvas.

225

Step 8

Mix the paint across the canvas

Step 9

Add green stems with a sweeping motion from the bottom to the top. It will make a point on the ends of the leaves. Then use the back of the palette knife to pick up the paint.

Step 10

You can get different shapes depending on which palette knife you use. Don't be afraid to experiment its fun!

Step 11

You can go back and add details with a paint brush. Here I chose a different shade of yellow to add to the base of the flowers then I went back and painted green stems and leaves. Every bit you add makes it more beautiful.

Step 12

Added the blue flowers with a little dot for the center.

Step 13

Adding purple flowers

Step 14

Painting the bumble bees. You paint three black lines and alternate with yellow and using a fine brush you add the antenna.

232

Step 15

Add two little white wings

Finished!

All framed. Just love how this one came out!

I have a teaching lesson on my YouTube channel called Dragonfly Corners you can follow along in its entirety.

The title is:

Textured Palette Knife Dandelions and Wildflowers Acrylic Painting

Enjoy!

Made in the USA
Columbia, SC
29 October 2024